MW00580842

TALES AND CUSTOMS OF THE ANCIENT HEBREWS

DAVID, THE SHEPHERD BOY

TALES AND CUSTOMS
OF THE
ANCIENT HEBREWS
for
YOUNG READERS

BY

EVA HERBST

ILLUSTRATED BY

MILTON HERBST

YESTERDAY'S CLASSICS

CHAPEL HILL, NORTH CAROLINA

This edition, first published in 2008 by Yesterday's Classics, an imprint of Yesterday's Classics, LLC, is an unabridged republication of the work originally published by A. Flanagan Company in 1903. For the complete listing of the books that are published by Yesterday's Classics, please visit www.yesterdaysclassics.com. Yesterday's Classics is the publishing arm of the Baldwin Online Children's Literature Project which presents the complete text of hundreds of classic books for children at www.mainlesson.com.

ISBN-10: 1-59915-292-4

ISBN-13: 978-1-59915-292-9

Yesterday's Classics, LLC
PO Box 3418
Chapel Hill, NC 27515

CONTENTS

DAVID

To-DAY, boys and girls, as we look about us, and see how we live and what we enjoy, let me tell you about some people who lived almost three thousand years ago. That seems a long, long time, as we look back, but there were many people on this earth as long ago as that. Some of these people were called Hebrews.

I am going to tell you how the Hebrews lived, and what some of them did. Now, you know, in all times men must have food to eat, and civilized people must have clothes to wear. So many of these people were shepherds and farmers. They raised thousands of sheep, to use the wool for clothing. There were no factories then, as there are now, and so the people themselves had to weave the cloth for their clothes.

The men who took care of the sheep were called shepherds. Among these shepherds could be found persons of every rank, from members of the king's family down to the poorest people. Even the daughters of the king sometimes tended the flocks. Each morning the shepherd led his sheep into the open pastures. At night he put them into a place surrounded by a fence. This place was called the fold. A rod was held up at the gate of the fold, and as the sheep passed under this they were counted, one by one. The shepherd led them to the wells to drink. These wells were dug in the ground.

1

They were covered, so that no one but the shepherd who had dug them should know where they were. The brim of the well was underground, and steps led down to it. The shepherd drew the water from the well and poured it into troughs for the flock.

In the country where the Hebrews lived water was very scarce. There was a wet and a dry season. During the wet season, which was also the cold or winter season, wells were sometimes dug and filled with snow and water. They were then covered over until the next warm, dry season, or summer. In the cold, wet season, the flocks were taken down into the valleys, and in the warm, dry season they were led into the mountains. The sheep were kept in the open air, day and night. This made their wool so much finer.

Sometimes the shepherds lived in tents. Some of these tents were small and were supported by three poles. The larger ones had seven or even nine poles to hold them up. The tents were oblong. Over the poles was a covering of cloth, made of goat's hair. The tent was fastened to the ground by means of cords and pegs. The larger tents were often divided into three parts. The women and children had the inside room; next came the men, and in the outside room were the servants and the young animals.

These tents had no floors but the bare ground. Carpets and mats were laid down and on these the people sat, as they had no chairs. They had pots, kettles and cups made of brass, and bottles made of leather. In the middle of the tent a small hole was dug in the earth-floor. Around this three stones were placed to form a triangle. Here the fire was kindled and pots were placed over it, resting upon the stones. In this way their cooking was done.

In the tent-poles were driven nails, on which the people hung their clothing and their weapons. The shepherds took their tents with them, as they roved from place to place. They carried them folded and laid upon their camels, oxen or donkeys.

They also built tabernacles. The four sides of a tabernacle were made of branches of trees placed close together, upright in the ground. The branches were bound together at the top, and there was a covering of leaves and branches over this. Sometimes over this covering flat stones were laid. These tabernacles were a protection against the heat and cold.

What made the people think of making these tabernacles? Why, Mother Nature gave them this idea. They saw trees about them, with the heavy foliage meeting and overlapping, and so they made their places of shelter in the same manner.

There were robbers in those days, and, so that the sheep could be guarded, a watch-tower was built near the tent. Some of the shepherds owned thousands of sheep. They often had goats, also. Not only was the wool of the sheep of use to them, but they used the milk of both sheep and goats for food. At sheep-shearing time the people had a great feast.

The shepherds were not always men, for often young boys were sent out to take charge of the sheep.

Now we shall hear of one of these Hebrew shepherd boys. His name was David. That was the only name by which he was called. He had been given this name when he was eight days old, for such was the Hebrew custom. David watched the sheep in the fields near the city of Bethlehem. Bethlehem is across the sea, in the Far East.

It would take us many weeks to travel to the beautiful country in which David lived. It was known for its fertile fields and rich pastures. Beautiful trees of many kinds grew there: among them were the palm, fir, cypress, fig, and olive. In the valley the air was fragrant with the sweet odor of flowers, which were everywhere to be seen.

David was a handsome boy, with bright eyes and long red hair. You would think his dress very queer if you could see him now. He wore a white garment of linen, called a tunic. It reached to his knees and was fastened around his waist with a leathern girdle. His arms, legs, and feet were bare. His head also was bare, and he carried in his hand a staff with a crook at the end. Hanging from his girdle was a shepherd's pouch, in which he carried food and other things. This pouch was made of kid's skin and had a strap fastened to each end.

As David watched his sheep there, day after day, out in the open air, he grew to be a strong, healthy boy. He was fond of using his sling, and many and many a smooth pebble was thrown from it. But do not think he spent all of his spare time in this way. He was never idle,

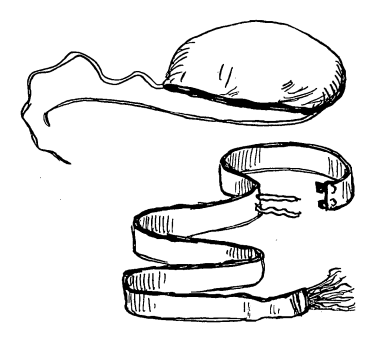

DAVID'S POUCH AND GIRDLE

but tried in many ways to learn, and to improve himself. He was alone among his flock, with the blue sky above him and the olive trees, with their green branches, about on the hills. Around him were the high mountains. All this beauty of nature made David feel very happy. So he sang and played upon his harp *(kinnor)*, which he always carried with him, and many hours of the day were spent in this way.

David played and sang so well that all people loved his music. It is said that even the sheep listened to his harp and followed their beloved leader about. When he grew to be a man, he also wrote beautiful songs, so that to this day we hear of David as the "Sweet Singer in Israel."

When David was about fourteen years old, as he was one day watching his sheep and playing upon his harp, a man came running to him. "David, come at once to your father's house," cried he. His father lived in Bethlehem.

Now let us go to the city, and learn why David has been sent for. See, there is a man coming toward Bethlehem. Who is he? He walks along, driving a heifer. When he comes near the wall, which surrounds and protects the city, he sees many men sitting at the gate. This is the meeting-place of the judges. They are talking about the affairs of the city. When the man comes nearer, the judges run to meet him. They wonder why he has come, for the man is Samuel, the great prophet.

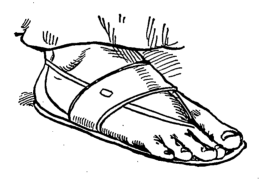

FOOT WITH SANDAL

The prophet in those days was at the head of all his people. Even the king always consulted him about his affairs. This prophet Samuel was an old man, with white hair and a long beard. He wore a long white woolen cloak over his tunic. On his feet were sandals. These were flat pieces of leather, bound to the sole of the foot with a strap. His head was covered with a band of linen. He carried a staff, and a long horn filled with oil.

The people asked Samuel why he had come. He said it was for a sacrifice, and he told them to get ready for it.

I hear some one ask: "What is a sacrifice?" I will tell you. Whenever the Hebrews wished to give thanks to God for his goodness, they offered to him whatever they thought the most valuable of their possessions. Sometimes they gave animals, as sheep, goats and cows, and sometimes fruit or grain. They gave them in this way: If it were a sheep or goat that was to be given, the man who offered the sacrifice led the animal to the altar. Here it was slain and some parts of it were burnt. When fruit or grain was offered it was laid upon the altar and burnt in the same manner. After the offering had been made there was a feast.

So the prophet told the people to go up on one of the hills near the city, where they would sacrifice to God. And this gave much joy to the people.

After Samuel had told the people this, he went to the home of Jesse, the father of David. Jesse was a weaver of carpets. When Samuel reached the place, he saw a square-looking house of one story. It was built of stones which were cut in squares. The house had no windows in front. That seems strange to us, but when I tell you how the house was built you will understand how this could be so.

There was a door, in the front, and when the

prophet knocked at it a servant opened it from the inside, by drawing back the wooden bolt. Jesse came forth and warmly greeted Samuel. As Samuel passed in to the porch, he saw the usual inscription on the door. This contained a prayer. Here, on the porch inside the house, the servant of Samuel sat on a seat which was placed there for those strangers who were not admitted any farther into the house. Here, also, the sandals were removed from Samuel's feet. His feet were then washed by Jesse. A guest's feet were usually washed by a servant, but when so great a man as a prophet came into the house, the master of the house thought it an honor to perform this duty. The roads of the country were dusty, and so it was necessary to wash the feet often.

Samuel passed through another door into the middle of the house. This part was the court. It was a large square place paved with marble. One could walk around the sides of the court under cover, and watch the fountain playing in the center. If you could have looked in here, on a day when there was a large crowd of people gathered together, for a wedding or some other happy event, you would have seen a covering of cloth, held up by ropes, over the whole court. This protected the people from the sun. All around the court were rooms, and you could have seen into them through the windows extending to the floor. The windows in the back rooms looked upon a large garden behind the house.

You would not have seen any glass in these windows, as they were screened only by a lattice of wood. When the cold weather came, the people could be seen putting up a sort of veil of cloth before the windows. You may wonder why their windows were left open, but when I tell you that the Hebrews at that time had no chimneys in their houses, you will understand that this had to be done, so that the smoke from their fires could escape. Do you think these people had stoves for heating, as we have? Their fireplace was a small space hollowed out in the center of the paved floor. In this was set a pot filled with burning coal or wood, and, as I have said before, the smoke escaped through the windows. When the fire burnt out, the heat was kept in the fireplace by a covering of carpet laid over a frame. In some houses there was no fire at all, for the weather was never very cold.

Do not these things seem strange to us? Yet if David, the shepherd boy, could come to our homes, our ways would seem just as strange to him.

When Samuel had gone into the house with Jesse, he invited Jesse and his sons to go with him to the sacrifice. So they got ready at once. They took off their dark woolen clothes. They washed, and then rubbed their bodies with oil. After this, they put on their white robes. White was always worn at a sacrifice, for white meant cleanliness and purity.

Samuel the prophet had been sent by God to choose one of the sons of Jesse to be the future king. So, at the place of sacrifice up on the hill, as the eldest son passed before the prophet, he looked so strong and manly that Samuel said to himself: "Surely, he is the one." But no, he was not the man to be chosen. Then, as the next son came up, "Nor is he the one," said the prophet. Nor was the third or the fourth the one, and at last, when the seven sons had passed before the great man, not one of them had been chosen as the king.

Then Samuel said to Jesse: "Have you no other son?" "Oh, yes," answered Jesse, "David, the beloved, but he is only a boy. He is tending the flocks." "Send, and fetch him," said Samuel, "for we will not sit down till he come hither." And now we know why David had been sent for.

David went at once, for he had been taught—as all Hebrew children were taught—to obey and respect his parents, before all other duties. As he passed along the road, here and there, he saw the people sitting under the fig trees, and he could hear the merry shouts of the children playing in the courts of the houses. As he approached those who were awaiting him, he was a "goodly sight to look upon." With his bright face all aglow, he stepped before the prophet.

Samuel knew at once that he had found the one for whom he had been sent. He said: "He is the one." He took the horn, and poured the oil on the head of David. Thus the boy was anointed to be a future king.

And Jesse and his sons sat with Samuel at the feast. After the feast, Samuel went back to Ramah, his home, and David continued to live the life of a shepherd, just as before.

Now, when Jesse and his sons went back to their home, it was evening. They saw the new moon rising above the hills. They knew by this that the next day would be the first day of the new month, and they knew, too, that when the new moon rose for the seventh month, they would hear the trumpet blow to tell the people a new year had begun.

HOUSE TOPS

As they came nearer to their home, they met a stranger. They took him home with them. He remained with them for the night. His beast of burden was taken care of. The next morning, as the man started on his journey, one of the sons went with him for a short distance.

When they entered the house, after coming from the place of sacrifice, they saw the table spread for the evening meal. What a strange table it was, to be sure—nothing but a round piece of leather, spread upon the floor! It had a cloth over it, to keep it clean. In the middle of this was a sort of stool. This stool supported a platter.

The men of the family sat around the table, with their legs crossed: some were on pieces of carpet, and some on cushions. There were no knives, forks or spoons to be seen. On the platter was the meat, which had been boiled in a copper kettle. Each person was given a piece of meat, which was put on his bread; thus the bread served as a plate. Of course, as there were no forks, people took up the meat and ate it with their fingers. You know, they always washed their hands before sitting down to a meal. In the same manner they ate beans, onions, lentils and cucumbers. If we could have eaten with them, we should have tasted a bit of salt in all they ate.

There were also cakes, raisins, figs and dates upon the table. A brass cup was placed before each person. Into this cup water was poured from a leathern bottle.

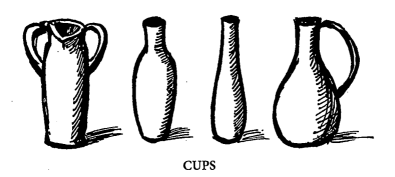

CUPS

Would you like to know how these leathern bottles were made? They were made by stripping off the skin of a goat or kid, from the neck downward. The skin was not ripped. The four legs were cut off. The holes thus left were sewed up. The hole left at the neck served as a spout, and was tied up to close the bottle.

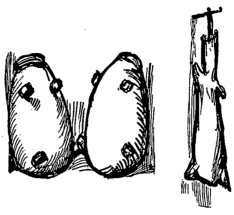

LEATHERN BOTTLES

The meat eaten by the Hebrews was the flesh of oxen, sheep and goats. Pigeons and fish also were used for food.

After the meal was over, David went with his father, up a flight of stairs, from the porch to the roof. You are surprised to hear this, and the roof, if we could have seen it, would have seemed the strangest part of the house to us. It was flat, so that one could walk about on it. It was a solid floor, made of coal, stones, ashes and gypsum pounded together. Often the roofs of these Hebrew houses were so close together that one could easily have stepped from one to the next. Some were made of earth, and here and there herbs and spears of wheat and barley could be seen springing up. The people did not fall off, because there was a wall built all around the roof. This was built according to a law among the Hebrews, and reached as high as a man's chest. A small room, in one corner of the roof, was used for the servants. Think how queer it would seem to us, to see people walking about on the roofs of the houses!

David walked with his father, to and fro, upon the roof, to enjoy the air. Jesse wished to talk to him alone. Crowds were passing in the narrow street below. Jesse announced to them that he would next day have a splendid feast at his home for the people. After praying to God up here, Jesse and David returned to their rooms below.

It was night. The lamp was burning in the room where David slept. This lamp was an oblong iron vessel, which had a round opening in the middle into which olive oil was poured. At one end was a small hole for the linen wick, and at the other end was a handle.

LAMP

Now the thick mattresses were taken from a box along the wall, where they were kept during the day. They were placed upon the floor and used as beds. The floors were clean, for you know the sandals were not worn in the house.

The Hebrews had, too, a sort of bed resembling a sofa. Sometimes this was ornamented with ivory, on the sides and back. Upon this bed were placed pillows stuffed with wool.

After all had lain down upon their beds, a dim light could still be seen, during the whole night.

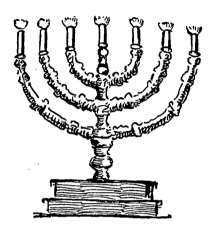

CANDLESTICK

Where was the mother of David all this time? The women of those days did not as a rule take their meals in the same room with the men, unless there was some great feast. So David's mother was with the other women of the home, in a room in the rear of the house.

Here, in these back rooms, we might have seen the women busily spinning, dyeing, weaving and sewing. For all the clothing was made in the home. The Hebrew home was a "hive of industry," among the rich and poor alike. Even the children were taught to be active and busy.

The women dressed in very much the same way

as the men. But their dresses were fuller and longer, and made of finer material, and their under-garments had sleeves. The women were fond of bright colors, and a dress of scarlet was commonly worn. The girdle, too, was of fine woven stuff. The Hebrew women wore turbans on their heads. They did not go out in public often, but when they did, they always wore a veil to cover the face. Gold and silver rings, bracelets and necklaces were worn by them. Just think of it—we have even read of women wearing rings around their ankles.

Besides the making of clothing, there was other work to be done in the home. For there the wheat and barley were ground into flour, and there the bread was baked.

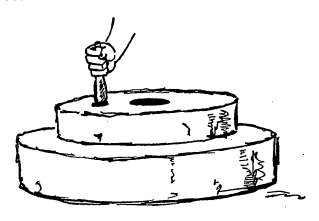

MILL FOR GRINDING FLOUR

Each family had its own mill. This was made by placing two round stones one above the other. The lower one was so fixed in the floor that it did not move around. It was higher in the center, and this high place fitted into a hollow place in the upper stone. There was a hole through the upper one, and into this hole the grain was poured. By means of a wooden handle, the upper stone was turned around on the lower one.

Thus the grain was broken up and ground into meal. As David went back and forth through the city, he could hear the noise of these mills in the houses. They were used every morning and evening, except on the Sabbath.

BASKET

Now, since you know how the flour was made, would you like to know how the Hebrews made their bread? The people of that time did not have all the different kinds of food that we have to-day, but in all ages people have eaten bread in some form.

To make the bread the flour and water were mixed in a wooden tray. Of course, each family owned an oven, where the bread was baked. Sometimes, this oven was only a hollow made in the earth. The bottom was paved with stones. When the oven was warmed, the fire was removed. Then the bread or cakes were placed on these hot stones, and the mouth of the oven was closed.

They also had a movable oven made of brick,

smeared with clay on the inside. The dough was put on the outside, like a plaster, and thus baked. The women of the household did most of this work.

Up to this time, you have heard nothing about the schools for the children. Well, there were no schools, outside of their homes. Do you think they learned nothing on this account? No, indeed, for the parents considered it a duty to teach the children themselves.

The girls, until they were married, spent all of their time with their mothers. They were not idle, but were taught all the useful things that must be done in a home. They were taught to spin, sew, embroider, and, of course, to cook. They also learned to sing and dance. Usually when they danced, they played upon an instrument called a timbrel. This was made of a round brass or wooden hoop, covered with a tightly drawn skin and hung round with small bells. It was held in the left hand and beaten with the right. The daughters did not go out on the streets very often, but once in a while they could be seen, with urns, carrying water from the wells.

The boys, likewise, until they were five years old, were under their mothers' care. Then their fathers took them in charge. They were taught reading and writing. And here again, how different their way was from ours!

They wrote on goat-skin or sheepskin, and sometimes on sheets of paper made of the papyrus plant. On this they wrote with black ink, using a sharp-pointed wooden instrument called a stylus. The writing

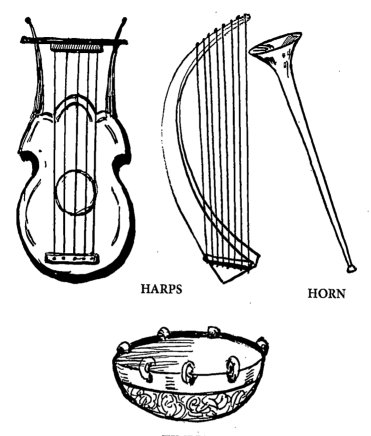

HARPS   HORN

TIMBREL

was from right to left. The lines were short, so that on each sheet there were written many separate columns. The sheets were not bound into books as we have them, but were joined together and rolled around a stick and sometimes around two sticks.

This roll of writing was called a scroll. In earlier times people also wrote upon stones.

Besides this, the boys were taught farming. They practised shooting with the bow and arrow, throwing with the sling, lifting heavy weights, and running races, to make them strong and healthy. But above all this, the history of their nation, and the love of God were impressed upon their minds. Usually the fathers and sons talked of these things on the Sabbath, as this was a day of rest.

SCROLLS

Jesse told David about the great men and women who had lived many years before. He told him what they had done for his people. He talked to him of the wisdom and goodness of God. He taught him that the love and fear of God was the beginning of all knowledge.

Now from all this we know that David, as a boy, was taught to be industrious, to obey and respect his parents, and, above all, to worship God.

MOSES

One Sabbath day, David sat with his father, in the garden behind their house. At their feet were beautiful flowers, and they sat in the shade of a fig tree, whose broad leaves and spreading branches made for them a cool resting-place on this warm day. From this tree they could pluck the juicy figs which they ate with their simple mid-day meal of milk, bread and honey. In another part of the garden many grape vines could be seen, and here, also, grew the vegetables. Near by was the cistern with its cool water.

Jesse read to David from a scroll. He read how the Hebrews had come to live in the land of Canaan. David was glad to hear these stories, and, as his father read or related them again and again, he learned to know much about his people. As they sat together on that bright day, Jesse told the story which David loved more than all others—the story of a great man who had done much for his people.

You will like to hear it, I know, as well as David did, so many, many years ago. This is the story Jesse told:

Long, long years ago, our people did not live in this country of Canaan. They lived in Egypt. Once a baby boy was born among them. The King of Egypt

21

had given an order that all Hebrew boys, as soon as they were born, should be thrown into the river. When this little boy came to live upon this earth, his mother, of course, loved him very dearly. She could not bear the idea of having him thrown into the dark river. She was very sad, and scarcely knew what to do.

She hid her dear little baby for three months, so that nobody might know about him, but you know babies are not always quiet; they will sometimes cry and make much noise. When the poor mother knew she could keep him concealed no longer, she said: "What shall I do? I cannot give him up." She thought about it for some time. Then at last, she said: "Now, I have a good plan."

She made a basket of rushes. It was coated with pitch, so that the water would not leak through. It looked just like a little cradle. And now, when the basket was finished, what do you think she put into it? Why, her dear little boy. She told her daughter Miriam to place the basket, with the baby in it, among the bulrushes that grew along the river.

After Miriam had done this, she stood behind the trees near by, to watch the precious basket. She had not been there long, before she saw the king's daughter and her maids coming along. They often bathed here, in the river. As they came near, the princess saw something strange among the rushes. "Go, see what that strange thing is," she cried to her maids, "and bring it to me."

One of the maidens then lifted the basket from the water, and carried it to the princess. How delighted she was, when she saw the wee baby! She exclaimed: "What a handsome baby! He must be a Hebrew child. I will save him from the river, and keep him as my own son."

Then Miriam came forward, and asked the princess if she cared to have her get a nurse for the baby. The princess bade her do so, and Miriam went quickly for her own mother. Her mother came, and as she took her boy into her arms once more, how happy she was! Now she knew his life would be saved. The princess commanded her to take the baby to her own home, and said she would pay her to care for him, until he should be old enough to live at the palace. The princess named the baby Moses, for this name means "drawn out of the water."

When Moses was still a young child, he was taken from his own humble home to the home of the princess. He was so handsome, it is said, that men would turn and look at him as he passed them at their work. He seemed brighter than other boys of his age.

The princess loved him as though he were her own son. She took him to her father, Pharaoh, the king. He, also, became very fond of the boy. He had him taught and trained, just as though Moses had been the grandson of the Egyptian king.

As a child, Moses wore no clothes, as was the custom among the Egyptians. He had several people to care for him when he went out. He was taken into the streets in a wheeled vehicle. Sometimes he was taken for a sail in a boat, on the river.

In Egypt the education of a boy trained the body as well as the mind. The boys played such games as wrestling, fighting with single sticks, ball, and lifting and swinging heavy bags of sand over their heads.

Besides being trained in these games, Moses was carefully educated in all that was known at that time. Pharaoh sent for the wisest teachers in the land. Moses began by learning to read and write the Egyptian language. He learned the Hebrew language, also. After this he studied arithmetic and learned the multiplication tables. He also studied music. During his youth he had teachers at the court of Pharaoh, but as he grew older he was sent to the university, where he was taught law. He learned about the stars, and also about medicine. He was trained to be a soldier and a leader. You will hear how this helped him in after years. You see, the king wished to make Moses a ruler in the land, next to himself.

But while he was taught all these things, there was one teacher whose words were more to him than all else that he learned. This teacher was his own mother. Remember, she was the nurse chosen by the princess. As Moses was still young when taken to Pharaoh's court, his mother went with him. When he was under her care she talked to him of many things which he did not hear from his other teachers. He heard of his own people, the Hebrews, who had now lived almost four hundred years in this land of Egypt. He learned how they had become slaves to the Egyptians, and how hard they were made to labor. So that Moses, although living in the Egyptian court, never forgot that he was a Hebrew.

When he grew to be a man, he went among his people to see how they lived. He saw them working as slaves in the brick fields. Some were digging the clay out of pits, and some were shaping the bricks. He observed how cruelly they were treated. Then he went back to the court. As he lay on his fine couch, in his beautiful room, all these sights came back to him. He thought: "How can I help my brethren? Can I do nothing for them?"

One day, as he was walking in a lonely place, he saw an Egyptian treating a Hebrew very roughly. Moses became so angry that he struck the Egyptian, and killed him. When Moses found that he had killed the man, he was horrified. No one being in sight, he buried the body in the sand. This was all over so quickly that Moses scarcely knew what a terrible deed he had done, but it was soon known among the people, and Moses fled from the king's anger.

He wandered into the land of Midian. As he sat resting by a well, the daughters of the priest of Midian came to draw water from the well for their sheep. Some shepherds, who lived near by, tried to drive the maidens away, but Moses prevented the shepherds from doing this, and helped the maidens to water their flocks.

They went home and told their father about the stranger. Jethro, their father, sent for him to come to his home. After this, Moses made his home with Jethro and tended his flocks. He married one of Jethro's daughters and lived many years among these people.

Though far away from his own people, Moses

still thought of them, and longed to save them from the hard life they were leading. One day, as he was tending his flocks on the mountain side, he saw a strange sight. There, in a bush near by, a bright fire was burning. As it burned, strange to say, the leaves and branches were not even scorched by the flames. He approached nearer to it. A voice seemed to call to him: "Moses, Moses, come not nearer; take thy shoes from off thy feet: this is holy ground."

Then Moses removed the sandals from his feet, and listened to the voice. It said: "Go to Pharaoh, and lead the people of Israel out of Egypt. Bring them to this mountain, and offer sacrifices to me, for I am their God. Tell them I am the God of Abraham, Isaac and Jacob."

But Moses answered: "Who am I, that I should go to Pharaoh?"

God said: "I will be with you."

Then Moses replied: "I cannot do this. The people will not believe in me."

The voice then said: "Cast your staff upon the ground." Moses did so, and the staff changed into a serpent. Moses was afraid, and ran from the serpent. But again the voice called to him: "Take hold of it by the tail." Moses took hold of the tail, and as he touched it, the serpent changed into his staff again. God said: "If the people will not believe you, show them this sign. If they will not then believe you, I will cause other wonders to happen in the land."

Still Moses did not wish to go. He said: "I cannot

talk well." Then God said: "I will tell you what to say. Is there not Aaron, your brother? He will come to meet you. He shall go with you, and he shall speak to the people for you. Go, and take your staff with you, to show the signs."

At last, Moses went to Jethro and asked to be allowed to go back to Egypt, to see if his relatives were still alive. Then Moses set out on his journey. On the way, he met his brother Aaron, who had been sent by God to meet him. They were happy to see each other again. Moses kissed his brother, and told him of God's command.

They went into Egypt and called the elders of the people together. Then Aaron told them what had happened, and why Moses had returned. It made the people joyful to hear all this, and they thanked God for his goodness. The two brothers went to Pharaoh, the King of Egypt. They asked him to let the Children of Israel (as the Hebrews were sometimes called) go, for three days, to offer sacrifices to their God, on the mountains. But the king would not allow them to go.

After this, the Hebrews were made to work even harder than before. This made them angry with Moses, as they thought he was the cause of this new trouble. Moses and Aaron went to the king again. Aaron threw down his staff before Pharaoh, and it was changed into a serpent, but the king only said: "No, the people shall not go."

Once again Moses and Aaron stood before Pharaoh. This time they were by the river. The king still refused to let the people go. Moses, to show the power of God, told Aaron to lift his staff above the river; Aaron did so and all the water was turned into blood. Now this was the first of the ten plagues which were to fall upon the Egyptians. Not only here in the river, but everywhere in Egypt—in the wells and even in the houses—the water was turned into blood. The fish in the river died. But even this did not change the king.

Then Aaron, as he was bid, again stretched his staff over the river. At this, thousands of frogs came up, out of the water, all over the land. At last Pharaoh was frightened. He sent for Moses and Aaron. He said: "Ask your God to take away these frogs, and I will let the people go." But as soon as the frogs were no longer to be seen, he forgot his promise.

And God told Moses to have Aaron strike the ground with his staff. Aaron did so, and the land was covered with vermin. They were upon every man and every beast. The wise men said: "This is the hand of God." Still the heart of Pharaoh did not feel for the people. Next, God sent great swarms of flies, and they filled the land. They settled upon everything—indoors and out of doors. They were all over Egypt, except in that part of the country where the Hebrews lived. Again Pharaoh sent for Moses. He said: "Offer sacrifices to your God in this land." Moses answered that this could not be done. "Then," replied Pharaoh, "go, but do not go far from here." But, as soon as the flies had disappeared, he took back his promise.

Moses told Pharaoh that if he would not let the

people go, all the cattle in Egypt should die. And this happened, as Moses had said. Only the cattle of the Hebrews did not die.

Next, all the Egyptians were covered with boils. Then a terrible storm of thunder and lightning was sent. The hail came down and killed the crops; it broke the trees; it killed every man and beast in the field. The storm was so dreadful that Pharaoh again sent for Moses, but when the hail had ceased to come down, the king's heart was as hard as before.

The next plague came in this way: the whole country was full of locusts. In the trees, in the houses, in every nook and corner, these locusts were found. They ate up everything which the hail-storm had left. Then Pharaoh sent for Moses and Aaron, and said to them: "I have sinned against your God and you. Take away the locusts." Moses begged God to take away the locusts, and a strong wind came and blew them into the sea. Then, just as so many times before, Pharaoh forgot his promise.

Now there came a terrible darkness over the land. For three days it was so dark that the Egyptians could not even see one another. They could not leave their beds. But there was light where the Hebrews lived. Again Pharaoh sent for Moses. "Go ye," he said, "and offer sacrifices to your God. Only, your flocks and herds must remain behind." Moses said the people should not go without their cattle. Pharaoh then cried: "Get thee from me. See my face no more." Moses answered: "I will not see thy face again."

Thereupon the Hebrews began to get ready to go out of the land. At God's command Moses told them to ask the Egyptians for jewels and silver and gold. And the Egyptians gave them many valuable things. Moses bade each Hebrew to kill a lamb, and splash the blood upon the lintel of his door. Thus the homes of the Hebrews were to be known from those of the Egyptians. This was on the night of the fourteenth of the first month, called Nisan. Moses told the people that, forever after, a feast should be held on the anniversary of this night, in memory of God's goodness. This should be called the "Feast of Passover."

That night, a more terrible plague than all the other ones visited the Egyptians. At midnight, wailing was heard in all parts of the land, for in every home, in palaces as well as in the poorest huts, the first-born son lay dead. Not one person had died among the Children of Israel. This was the tenth plague sent by God upon the Egyptians. Then Pharaoh was so frightened that he called for Moses and Aaron, and cried: "Rise, and take the people and all their belongings. Go out of the land and serve your God."

The Egyptians helped them in their preparations, for they thought that unless the Hebrews went, they themselves would all die. The Children of Israel took with them all they could carry. Think what preparation was necessary! Think of a crowd of about six hundred thousand men, besides the women and children, leaving the country at one time! What a long procession! How many, many people, and how many cattle and beasts of burden! They carried with them their tents, also. They were hurried away so quickly that the dough for their bread was was not yet leavened—that is, it had not had time to rise—so they carried "the unleavened dough, in kneading-troughs, bound up in their clothes, upon their shoulders."

Their departure from Egypt was on the night of the first full moon, after the winter was over. The days were growing longer, and the time of year was the most pleasant for traveling. At night the people slept upon their cloaks, which they spread upon the ground. They took a long way through the wilderness.

Some time after they had gone, Pharaoh was sorry that he had allowed the Hebrews to depart. He sent his mighty army, together with hundreds of two-wheeled chariots, after them.

As the Hebrews were close upon the Red Sea, they saw the Egyptian army coming in pursuit of them. They were greatly frightened. They became angry with Moses, and asked why he had brought them there to die. Moses said: "God will take care of you." At this, he raised his staff over the sea. A strong east wind blew all night, and the water of the sea divided. Then the Hebrews passed over on the dry sand, in the middle of the sea, with the water forming a wall on each side. A pillar of light in front showed them the way, while a dark cloud behind hid them from their enemies.

Pharaoh's chariots and the army rushed on to overtake them. The wheels of the chariots sank in the sand, as the horses dashed into the sea. The wind died away; the water rushed back into its place, covering chariots, horses and men. Not one Egyptian was left.

When the people of Israel saw what had happened, they were very thankful to God for their safe delivery from slavery. Moses sang words of praise to God, and all the Children of Israel joined in this song of praise. Miriam, the sister of Moses, was with them. She it was, you will remember, who years before had placed the little cradle by the river. Miriam and the other women took their timbrels in their hands, and they played and danced, as she, also, sang beautiful words of praise to God.

MOSES AND MIRIAM REJOICING

How happy they were! For this was their day of deliverance. And the Children of Israel, for all time to come, will bless Moses, who, with the help of God, delivered them from their bondage.

THE STORY OF RUTH

I am sure you all love to hear your parents talk to you of what their grandmothers and grandfathers did when they were young, so many years ago. So David loved to hear of his great-grandmother Ruth, who was known as the noblest and best of all Hebrew women.

Now, at one time, there had been a dreadful famine in Bethlehem. There lived there the family of Elimelech, his wife Naomi, and their two sons. When the famine came, they no longer had bread to eat, so they went into a strange country, and, soon after, the father died. Here the sons found wives, one of them being Ruth, the great-grandmother of David. They lived together happily, for some years; then both sons died, and Naomi was left very poor. She said: "I shall go back to my own people at Bethlehem. They will help me, for God has again blessed them with bread."

Then the daughters-in-law said they would go with her. All three started on the journey, but, after they had gone some distance, Naomi begged the others to return to their mothers' homes, where they would fare better than they would in a strange land. The young women felt very sad as they thought of leaving Naomi, and when she kissed them good-by they wept. They said they would not leave her. But Naomi still urged them, and at last the older of the two women kissed her mother-in-law again, and returned to her own home.

Ruth still clung to Naomi. She said: "Urge me not to leave thee, for whither thou goest, will I go: and where thou lodgest, will I lodge. Thy people shall be my people, and thy God, my God."

So the two women traveled on to Bethlehem. The name of this city—"House of Bread"—seemed rightly given, at the time these women found their way to a large farm near the city, for it was harvest time, and they saw the farmers busily gathering in the grain, which was very plentiful.

Naomi had no money to buy food, so Ruth went into the field. Here she saw the men and maidens working. She asked to be allowed to glean after the reapers. The grain was cut with the sickle, and bound into bundles which were called sheaves. As the reapers gathered the sheaves of grain, the stray ears which fell from them were picked up by Ruth. This was called gleaning. The men let her do this, as they wished to be kind to a stranger. Besides it was a law to allow the poor to glean.

When Boaz, the owner of the field, saw her, and learned who she was, and what a good daughter-in-law she was to Naomi, he told the men to help her—to let her have as much grain as she could carry. When she asked why he was so kind to her, Boaz said: "I have heard of your goodness. I have heard what you have done for your mother-in-law."

When it was time for the reapers to rest and eat

RUTH AND BOAZ

the mid-day meal, Boaz sent for Ruth. He asked her to join them. After she had eaten the parched corn, and the bread dipped in vinegar, she still had a share to take to Naomi. Thus she gleaned all day, and when she beat out with sticks what she had gleaned, she found she had an ephah, which was about a bushel, of barley.

She returned to Naomi, and told her what had happened. Naomi said: "Boaz is our kinsman. He is still the kind man he always was."

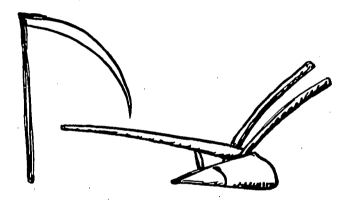

PLOW AND SICKLE

After this Ruth gleaned each day in the field, with the other maidens.

Now that you have seen these people all busily working on this large farm, let us go back and learn when the seed was sown, and how the work was done at that time. On these farms men and women, rich and poor, worked alike. Even kings, it is said, sometimes put their hands to the plow. The plow used in preparing the soil for the seed was easily lifted in one hand. It was a simple implement of wood, without wheels. It was so light that it made only a trifling furrow. Oxen and donkeys were used to draw the plow. The ground was leveled with a harrow. Spades and shovels were also used.

Now when Ruth came to this farm, it was the first season, or harvest time. The Hebrew year was divided into six seasons. The first season began in April and extended to the middle of June. The second season, summer or the time of fruits, began in June and ended in August. The weather was then so hot that people slept under the open sky. From the middle of August to the middle of October was the hot season.

During all this time—from the middle of April to the middle of September—there was no rain. This was the dry season. During May, June, July and August not a cloud could be seen. Think what it would mean to us to be without rain for five months! But the earth was not dry, as the dew was so heavy, and the ground was watered by canals.

After this hot season came the seed-time, from October to December. This was the time when the seed was sown. The first rain began to fall in the latter part of ·October. This was called the "former" rain. The farmers looked for this rain, to do their planting. The weather was still warm; but soon it grew colder. Snow could be seen on the mountains at the end of this season. In November the leaves fell from the trees.

Then came winter, which lasted until the middle of February. In winter there was some ice, but it melted very quickly, while in the valleys it was so warm on bright days that the fields were covered with flowers. As winter passed away in February, the crops began to grow, and the trees again put forth their green leaves.

Next came the last season, or the sixth part of the year. This lasted from the middle of February to the middle of April. Now there was more rain, and it was called the "latter" rain. The weather grew warmer. Soon the grain was ready to be cut.

We have already heard of the Feast of Passover. When the harvest-time began, which was also the beginning of this feast, a sheaf of barley was burnt as an offering to God. Thus the Hebrews offered the first-fruits of the harvest as a thank-offering to God, for the supply of grain which had been given them. Nothing raised on the farm could be eaten, nor could a sickle be put to the grain, until the offering was made.

Then the reaping commenced. First the barley, then the wheat, was cut. The grain was carried to the threshing-floor in wagons. These wagons had two wheels, and would look like carts to us. On a rising ground in the field was the threshing-floor. Here the grain was beaten with a roller. It is said that, even now, some of the old threshing floors are still to be seen. The threshing-machines of the Hebrews were made of wood, with iron teeth below, to force out the grain, and to cut up the straw. They were drawn by oxen.

The grain was separated from the chaff and fine-cut straw by winnowing; that is, by tossing it up with a spoon-shaped wooden implement against the wind. Then the grain was further cleared by passing it through a sieve. At last the grain was stored in a granary, which was sometimes only a cave or pit and sometimes a barn.

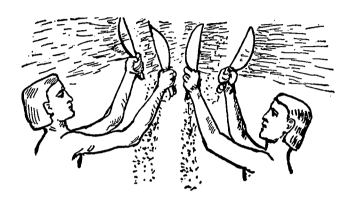

WINNOWING GRAIN

When the harvest-time—which lasted seven weeks—was over, there was another feast. This was Pentecost, or the Feast of the Harvest. Once again there was an offering, but this time it consisted of two loaves of bread, made of the new meal. There was dancing and singing at the feast.

Another feast of this kind was held in October, at the in-gathering of the fruits. This festival lasted eight days. The people erected booths of green boughs, to remind them of the tabernacles in which their ancestors lived in the wilderness. So this was called the Feast of Tabernacles.

Besides the grain, the farmers raised flax, cotton

and vegetables. They also had large orchards. The sides of the hills and mountains were covered with vineyards.

Boaz had now planted and reaped for six years, but the next year he would not plow or sow. Why was this? Because the Hebrews felt that the land belonged to God. They felt that it was theirs only for the enjoyment of what the soil gave them. To remind the people of this every seventh year was made a year of rest for the land. During this "Sabbatical" year no seed was sown, and all that grew was given to the poor.

After Boaz and the harvesters had finished their threshing, and Ruth had gleaned each day, they had a merry time of feasting, singing and dancing. Then it was that Naomi—planning to do something for the welfare of Ruth—bade her tell Boaz of her kinship to him.

There was a custom among the Hebrews which required the nearest kinsman of the dead husband to marry the widow, to keep the property from going to others. Boaz was pleased to hear that Ruth was related to him, and wished to make her his wife, but he knew that Ruth had a nearer relative, to whom this right belonged. He told Ruth to go home to Naomi, and he would see what could be done.

So the next day Boaz went to the open space in front of the gates of the city. This was the place where the elders met, to discuss the affairs of the city. Boaz knew he would meet his kinsman there. He called ten witnesses to listen, as he laid the matter before the man. He said: "The land that belonged to our relative Elimelech must be redeemed."

The man was willing to redeem the land, but when he heard that if he did that he must also make Ruth his wife, he said: "I cannot do that, but will give my rights to Boaz." He then drew off his shoe and handed it to Boaz, which meant that a bargain had been made. It was the same as a shake of the hand among us.

Thereupon Boaz and Ruth were married. Naomi was very happy for the sake of Ruth, who had been so good to her. All the people rejoiced, and hoped she would be happy. Thus Ruth was rewarded for her goodness.

Ruth had a son, and this son was the father of Jesse, and thus David became the great-grandson of this noble woman.

JOSEPH EXPLAINING PHARAOH'S DREAMS

THE STORY OF JOSEPH

We have heard before that the Hebrews were called "Children of Israel." They were so called because they were descended from Jacob. For God had given the name of "Israel" to Jacob, and so all the people who were descended from Jacob were called the "Children of Israel."

Jacob lived in Canaan. He lived long before Moses was born. He owned hundreds of sheep and cattle, and many droves of camels and donkeys. He was the father of twelve sons. Ten of his sons had grown to be men, while the youngest was still a baby, and the next to the youngest a tall lad.

Jacob seemed to love this lad, whose name was Joseph, more than all his other sons. The older sons did not like this, and did not speak kindly to Joseph. He told their father whatever wrong he saw his brothers do. This, also, made his brothers feel bitter toward him.

One day Joseph said: "What do you think I dreamed last night?" His brothers answered: "We do not care about your dreams"; but he told them the dream. "We were all in the harvest-fields," said he, "among the sheaves of grain, when it seemed that my sheaf stood up straight, while your sheaves seemed to bow down to mine."

His brothers were very angry and said: "Do you think you will reign over us?" They did not like this dream.

A few days after this Joseph again said: "I had a still stranger dream last night." They did not wish to hear him tell this, but the lad related the dream to them and to their father, Jacob. "It seemed," said he, "that the sun, moon and eleven stars all bowed down to me." This dream pleased the brothers still less, and now his father said sharply to him: "What, shall I and your mother and your brothers bow down to you? For by the sun and moon you mean your parents, and by the stars whom do you mean but your brothers?"

But after Jacob had thought more about it, he was pleased with this dream. It seemed to him that it meant great happiness for Joseph, and he loved him more than ever.

After the fruit had been gathered in, Jacob's older sons led their flocks to Shechem. Here there were good pastures for the sheep. This was fifty miles away from Hebron, where they lived. Joseph missed his brothers and their sheep. His father heard nothing from them, for a long time. One day he said to Joseph: "I wish I could hear how your brothers are getting along. It is a long time since we have heard from them." Then Joseph replied: "Let me go to them." Joseph was only a boy, and Jacob knew that there was danger from wild beasts on the way. But he knew, too, that Joseph was brave, although so young, and he was willing to let him go.

Joseph was soon ready. So he started on his

44

journey. He had on his simple dress, like the one David wore. He carried his leathern bottle, full of water. Of course, his shepherd's pouch, with food, he also had, for it would take him some days to travel so far. He also wore a beautiful coat, which his father had given him. It was a coat of many colors, woven of fine linen, and fastened with a fine leathern girdle. Perhaps he carried his sandals, for the way was long, and there were stones and rough places on the road.

Jacob kissed Joseph, as he bade him good-by, and hoped God would bless him on his way. Joseph's mother was not there to see him, for she had died a year before. Her grave was over the hills, in Bethlehem, not many miles away.

Joseph went on for several days. When he reached the place where he thought he would find his brothers, he looked about him. "Where are they? What can have happened to them?" thought Joseph, for not a man or a sheep was to be seen. Only the lonely field, without a sign of life, was about him. He was very much troubled. "What shall I do now?" thought he.

Just then, a man came near. "Have you seen the sons of Jacob, with their flocks, near here?" asked Joseph. "Yes," answered the man, "they were here for a long time, but now they have gone away. I think they have gone to find fresh pastures for the sheep." He then told Joseph the way to reach them. Joseph would not return to his father without some news of his brothers: so, although tired and hungry, this brave youth again started on. He walked some distance, and on coming to a green hill, saw the sheep grazing.

Let us see what his brothers had been planning to do, and why they went so far away from home. They hated their brother, and, terrible as it seems, wished to kill him. As he was still some distance away, one of the brothers said: "See, who is this coming to us?" They looked and saw Joseph, with his beautiful coat over his shoulders, coming toward them. "See," said one of them, "it is our brother, the Dreamer." For this was the name they had given him. "Now," said they, "we have the chance to do as we like with him. Let us kill him."

Most of the brothers did not seem to realize what a terrible deed this would be—to take the life of this youth, who had done no wrong to any one. But the thought filled Reuben, the eldest brother, with horror. "Do not, my brothers, be guilty of such a deed!" he pleaded, but they did not listen to him. So when he found they still meant to kill Joseph, he said: "Do not shed blood, but put him into a pit in the ground, and there let him die." The others thought this was the best plan.

When Joseph came up to them, he called: "How are you, my brothers? Our father sent me to see you." They said: "You are no brother of ours." Then the coat was taken away from him, and they put him into the pit. There was no water in it. Reuben then went away. The rest of the brothers sat down, to eat their meal of bread and parched corn. They still thought of Joseph in the pit.

One of the men, looking up, exclaimed: "Behold, who are coming this way?" In the distance, men and camels were seen coming toward them. "It is a caravan. The merchants are coming this way," said they.

The camels were usually in lines of seven. A servant led the first one; the second was fastened to the first one by a rope, the third to the second, and so on, following one behind the other. The leader of the caravan was always first, as he knew the way. Sometimes the men sat upon the backs of the camels, with a cloth under them for a saddle.

These caravans traveled across the country. The men traded, bought and sold goods. They traded what they raised in their own country for other things which were raised in other lands. They carried their measures and weights about with them. Their weights were stones, which they carried in bags. They bought and sold their goods, as being worth a certain weight of silver. Gold was not used in trading, as it is now with us. The coin principally used was the "shekel" and was worth about sixty cents in our money.

As the merchants often traveled a great distance, they carried with them such things as they might need. If we had seen them unpack their loads, we might have seen a mattress, a coverlet, a piece of leather (which made their table) and a few pots and kettles of copper. We think they must also have carried their leathern bags, their tents, lamps and food. At night they carried a lighted torch on a pole, so that no one of the caravan should be lost.

When Joseph's brothers saw the merchants approaching, one of them said: "Of what good will it be to us, if we kill our brother? Let us sell him to these men, for then the blood of our own brother will not be on our hands."

When the merchants came up to them, Joseph was taken from the pit. The merchants were asked how much they would give for Joseph. "We will give you twenty pieces of silver for him," said one of the men. So Joseph was sold to the men as a slave, and taken down into Egypt, together with the rest of the slaves whom they had.

While all this had been going on, Reuben was away looking for a lost lamb. When he returned to the tent, it was night. He went at once to the pit, intending, when his brothers were not there, to take Joseph out and thus save his life. As he looked into the dark hole, he could see no one. Then he called: "Joseph, Joseph," but no answer came. Now he knew that Joseph was no longer there. He feared that he was dead. He went to his brothers, who told him what they had done. Reuben was glad to hear from them that Joseph was still alive.

The brothers took Joseph's coat, and after tearing it and dipping it into blood, carried it to their father. "See, we have found this," said they. "When Jacob saw the well-known coat, all torn and red with blood, he thought some wild beast had killed his beloved son. Weeping bitterly, he cried: "My son is dead. I shall weep for him till I die." After the brothers saw how much their father felt the loss of Joseph, they were very, very sorry for what they had done, but it was then too late to call him back.

The merchants took Joseph to Egypt. There he was sold as a slave to a man who was the head cook for Pharaoh, the king. As soon as this cook discovered what a bright young man Joseph was, he had him educated; he treated him better than the other slaves; he also gave him charge of his house. Thus, Joseph grew to be a learned man. Once the wife of this cook told him that Joseph had not treated her well. Now this was not true, but Potiphar, the cook, believed his wife, and put Joseph into prison.

Here he fared better than the rest of the prisoners. For the keeper of the prison saw that Joseph was careful about his work, and that he was different from the other prisoners. He was friendly with some of the prisoners. One day, the king's butler, who was also in prison, told Joseph that he had had a strange dream. After hearing the dream, Joseph told him to be of good hope, for in three days he would be released from prison. In prison with them was the king's baker, also. He, too, had a dream. He was anxious to tell it to Joseph. After hearing it, Joseph said: "I do not like to tell you bad news, but your dream shows that you will be put to death in three days." And it happened just as Joseph had said; for the butler was set free from prison, and the baker was hanged. Joseph, however, remained in prison for two years after this.

One night, Pharaoh, the king, had two dreams. They seemed very strange dreams. He asked all the wise men in Egypt what they meant, but the wise men could not tell the meaning of them. Pharaoh was greatly troubled. Then it was that the king's butler thought of Joseph. It seems that he had not thought of him since he left the prison two years before. He told Pharaoh how Joseph had explained his dream in prison, and how it had come to pass. The king quickly sent for Joseph.

When Joseph had shaved himself, and put on his best clothes, he went before the king. Pharaoh said to Joseph: "I have had two dreams, and not one of the wise men can tell me what they mean. It is said that you can tell the meaning of a dream, as soon as you have heard it."

"I cannot, myself, do it," said Joseph, "but God will help me, and will tell me what your dreams mean."

Then the king related the first dream to him. He said: "In my dream, I seemed to be standing on the bank of the river Nile. I was watching the water, as it flowed along, when suddenly out of the water came seven large, fat cows. These cows began to feed peacefully in the meadow. Again I saw seven cows come out of the river, but these were lean and ugly. I had never seen cows so ugly-looking before. As soon as these lean cows saw the seven fine ones, they ran after them, and ate them all up; and even after eating the other ones, the lean cows did not seem to grow any fatter. This was strange to me. As I was watching them, suddenly I awoke. Soon, I slept again."

"I dreamed a second time, but this time I saw seven heavy ears of grain growing out of one stalk; then seven lean ears came out. These were blasted by the hot east wind, but they ate up the good ears. Wondering, I stood looking at the strange sight, when, suddenly, I awoke, and found it all a dream. Now, tell me, if you can," said the king, "what is the meaning of these strange things."

Joseph thought a moment and said: "Both dreams have but one meaning, O Pharaoh. The fat cows and full ears of grain mean seven good years. The lean cows and the lean ears mean seven bad years. Now this is what the dreams show: there are coming seven years of plenty in the land of Egypt, but after that will come seven dreadful years of famine, when nothing can be grown. Then all that has been in the land in the time of plenty will be eaten up. All the land will sink under the great and terrible famine.

"And now," continued Joseph, "since you have had both dreams during the same night, it is certain that these things will happen in this land. O King, seek some man to take charge of the land. Let him see to it that now, as the time of plenty is here, part of the grain be stored away. Then, when the time of famine shall come, there will be enough food to save the people from starvation."

Pharaoh was pleased with Joseph, and thought this good advice, so he asked his courtiers whom he should choose to do this work. The king said to Joseph: "Since you know all this, and no man seems wiser than you, I will make you, next to myself, the ruler over the land of Egypt. You then shall manage this work." The courtiers were greatly pleased with this. The king took a ring from off his finger, and gave it to Joseph. He also put a gold chain around Joseph's neck. He gave him clothes of fine linen. Then Joseph rode through the city in the royal chariot. The king proclaimed to the people: "Joseph shall be next to me in power. He shall rule over the land. All men shall do as he bids."

Now, at that time, there was great plenty in the land, so Joseph went to work at once. He built granaries, and collected the grain. He went about the country, telling the people what to do. There were larger crops raised on the farms during those years than ever before. He did not allow anything to be wasted. They stored away in the granaries so much wheat and corn that it could not be measured. All the storehouses were filled.

Then came the years of famine. Nothing grew on the farms. Everything seemed dead. The crops all failed, year after year. The people cried for food. Then Pharaoh sent them to Joseph. Joseph opened his storehouses, and the land of Egypt was saved. The famine spread far and wide, all over the world. People and animals were dying of starvation everywhere. When it became known throughout the world how wise Joseph had been, people went to Egypt to buy their food.

One day, ten strange men came to buy corn from Joseph. Joseph looked at them and drew back surprised, for who do you think they were? None other than his own brothers, who had sold him into Egypt! The men, however, did not recognize their long-lost brother. They bowed down before him.

"From whence do you come?" roughly asked Joseph. "We have come from Hebron to buy food, as there is a famine in our country," they answered. "No," said Joseph, "you are spies; you have come to find out about our land, and then you will go back and tell about it to your people." The men were much frightened. "Surely, we have come only for food," they said. "We are all sons of one father." "Where is your father?" Joseph then asked. "He is at home, and our youngest brother is with him," they replied. "We had another brother, but he is no longer living."

Then Joseph acted as though he were very angry. "You must prove to me that you are not spies. Send one of your brothers home, to bring back your youngest brother. The rest of you will be put into prison. Thus, I shall find out if what you say is true."

The men were put into prison. After three days Joseph said to them: "Go home, now, with your provisions, but leave one brother here with me. Then bring back your youngest brother, when you come again." The brothers talked among themselves, saying that they were now being punished for their treatment of Joseph, years before. When Joseph heard them, he felt so sad that he went out of the room, to weep aloud. After this, he kept Simeon, one of the brothers, and sent the rest to their home. He filled his brothers' sacks with provisions.

On their way home, the men stopped to feed their donkeys. On opening his sack, one of the brothers cried: "See what I have found!" And looking into the sack, what did they see? There was the money which he had paid for the grain. They were all badly frightened, and hurried home to tell their father about it, and when each man, on opening his sack, found his money, they were even more troubled.

They then told Jacob what the Egyptian ruler had asked of them. When he heard that they were to take Benjamin, the youngest brother, to Egypt with them, he cried: "Joseph is gone; Simeon is gone; and now you would take my youngest son away. All things seem to go wrong with me." Reuben, the eldest son, said to his father: "You may kill my two sons, if we do not bring Benjamin back to you. Trust him to me; I will take care of him." But Jacob would not let his youngest son go, for he felt that he could not live without Benjamin.

After a time, the famine grew worse. Jacob's family was again in need of food. The grain was all used up. Jacob told his sons to go to Egypt for more food. They would not go without Benjamin. Jacob was much troubled. He said: "Why did you tell the man you had another brother?" Judah, another of the sons, answered: "You may do with me as you like, if we do not bring Benjamin back to you. Only let us go, for we shall soon starve, unless we have more food."

So Jacob, at last, when he found nothing else could be done, allowed Benjamin to go with the rest. He told them to take back the money found in the sacks. He also sent presents to Joseph.

Once again they stood before Joseph. When he saw them with Benjamin among them, he told his steward to take them to the palace—to get all ready for the meal which they were to take with him. On the way to the palace they told the steward about the money they had brought back to Egypt. The man said he knew nothing about the money in the sacks. When they went into the palace, their brother Simeon, who had been kept in prison, met them. The slaves washed their feet and fed their beasts. The men spread out their gifts, and happily waited for the ruler.

As Joseph came in he took their gifts, and said: "How is your father? Is he still alive?" They bowed to the ground, as they replied: "He still lives." Joseph looked at Benjamin and said: "Is this your youngest brother? God bless you, my son."

Joseph ordered the meal to be served. The brothers sat together at one table. Joseph sat at another one. In those days an Egyptian could not sit at the same table with people of another country. The brothers thought it very strange, when they went to the table, to be placed according to their ages. Thus, they feasted, and rested for the night.

The next morning they were very happy, as they started homeward with their sacks full of corn. They had not gone far, when a band of horsemen overtook them. "You have stolen a silver cup from the ruler," called one of them.

"Let him in whose sack the cup may be found be made a slave," said the brothers; so the sacks were opened and searched. There again the money was found, as before, and after searching all the other sacks they at last came to that of the youngest brother, and here what did they find? The brothers could scarcely believe their eyes, as they saw the cup taken from the sack of Benjamin. They were almost struck dumb.

Now Joseph had ordered the money, which they had paid for the corn, to be put into their sacks. He also had had his own silver cup put into the bag where it was afterward found, but the brothers did not know this. So their sacks were again placed upon their beasts, and together all the brothers returned to the city. Once more they stood before Joseph. They were so worried that they did not know what to do.

"What have you done?" said Joseph. "Did you not know that I should soon discover any wrong you might do?" Then Judah, the brother who had promised Jacob that he would care for Benjamin, spoke to Joseph. "The cup has been found in the sack of our youngest brother. Take me as a slave, in his place, for I cannot go home to my aged father without him. I could not bear to see my father so. He will die if Benjamin does not return to him, for he alone remains to cheer my father, since our other brother was taken away. So, I beg of you, let me stay, but let Benjamin go back to our father."

When Joseph heard his brother speak in this way, he could keep silent no longer. After his officers had gone from the room he wept aloud, and cried: "I am Joseph, your brother. Is my father still alive?" His brothers could not answer him, they were so amazed. Joseph put his arms around the neck of Benjamin. "Do not fear for what you did to me," he said. "It was God who sent me to Egypt. I was sent here to save my father's family in this great famine. So let us be happy and thankful that these things have happened in this way."

His brothers kissed Joseph, and all of them wept together. "Go back and tell our father all about me," said Joseph. "Tell him I am ruler of this land. Bid him come with you and your families to live here in Egypt."

When Pharaoh, the king, heard of the happy meeting between the brothers, he also bade them welcome to his country. He sent chariots and provisions to Jacob. Joseph gave new clothes to all his brothers, and to Benjamin he gave five suits of clothes and three hundred pieces of silver.

They set out for their homes, and Joseph went with them part of the way. Upon reaching their father's home, they said to him: "Joseph is still alive." Jacob did not believe them, but when he saw the wagons and chariots, which the king had sent to take them to Egypt, he knew the good news was true. Jacob said: "I shall see Joseph before I die."

All was made ready, and Jacob and his sons and their families departed from their homes. Joseph met them and gave them the best land in Egypt to live in. The king also met them, and bade them welcome to his country, so here the "Children of Israel" found new homes. They dwelt in the land for four hundred years, until Moses was sent to lead them out.

DAVID AND GOLIATH

Often, as David watched his flocks, there were very grave dangers to face, for there were many wild animals about. It is told how at one time a lion attacked his sheep, and he, with his own hands, killed the lion and saved a lamb which the lion had seized. At another time he killed a bear. So, by leading this kind of a life, facing such dangers, he became a strong, brave man. He also learned, by living in the open air, under the blue sky, alone with nature, to see the beauty in the world about him. He grew to love the earth as God had made it, and looked to Him as the Giver of all blessings.

When David was a young man, the Hebrews were at war with the Philistines. One day he was sent with bread and parched corn for his brothers, who were in the army. He took, also, ten pieces of cheese, as a present for their captain. In those days it was the custom for each soldier to provide for himself. And Jesse thought, since his sons had been away with the army so long, that they would be in need of food. A servant went with David, and they had a wagon and donkey to carry the provisions. David was glad to be sent on such an errand.

The army was encamped not many miles from Bethlehem. When David reached the battlefield, he hurried to the front. Here he saw the soldiers with their arms. They carried clubs, slings, and bows and arrrows. Not one of them, except the king and his son, carried a sword. Although still young, David longed to be of service to his country. He found that the Hebrew army was in great trouble. They dared not advance against the Philistines, on account of a mighty giant among them, who threatened the Hebrews.

This giant, Goliath, was ten feet tall. For more than forty days he had come out and dared the Hebrews to choose a man to fight with him. And no man among them was brave enough to face this terrible giant. But when David heard his taunting cry, he walked up to King Saul and said: "I will meet this giant face to face."

When Saul looked at him, so young, and with no weapons, he was much surprised. "You are not able to do this," he said, "you are but a lad." But when David told him of the life he had led, how he had killed wild animals, and how he believed he would win by his strength in God, the king gave his consent.

King Saul gave David his own armor and weapons. As David put them on, he found they were so heavy that he could not walk. He threw them off, and, unarmed, went to meet the giant. He picked up five smooth stones out of the brook, as he went, and put them into his shepherd's pouch.

Now see him—this bright-faced youth, in his simple white shepherd's dress, his staff in hand, and no weapons but his sling. See the great giant as David faces him.

On his head Goliath wore a bronze helmet, which

covered his head, but left his face bare. On his body he wore a coat of mail, made of small plates of copper. They were fastened on cloth or leather, and overlapped one another. This coat of mail is said to have weighed two hundred pounds. His legs were protected, from the knees to the ankles, by a copper covering called greaves. They were fastened by clasps around the ankles. He carried a spear with a handle of wood. The head of this spear was made of iron. It weighed eighteen pounds. At his side hung his sword, and over his shoulders was swung his javelin. Besides all this he had a shield, which was large enough to protect his whole body. It was made of hide, and stretched on a wooden frame made of metal. This was carried by another man, his shield-bearer.

HELMET, BREASTPLATE, AND BOW AND ARROW

Think of this terrible sight to look upon, and then think of this young boy daring to approach him! What a great difference there was between them—the one so large in body, and protected in every way; the other so strong in heart, but with no outward protection but his old friend the sling.

Goliath was very angry when he saw David wished to fight with him. "Come near," he cried, "and I will give your flesh to the wild beasts." "No," said David, "for I shall give *your* flesh to the wild beasts. You come armed, but I come in the name of the Lord."

Then David, whirling his sling around his head, threw the stone. The stone struck the great Goliath in the forehead; it sank to the bone, and the giant fell to the ground. Now David quickly ran up, and, seizing the giant's sword, cut off his head.

When the giant fell the Philistines fled. The Hebrew army pursued them, and gained a great victory. David was then brought before the king.

King Saul asked: "Who art thou?" "I am the son of Jesse, of Bethlehem," said David. The king would not allow him to return home that day.

When David, with the king, returned home from the battlefield, he took with him what he had taken from the giant. And from all the cities the women came out to meet the victors, they were so happy to see the army returning home again. They danced and sang a song of victory, as they beat their tambourines and struck their triangles, just as Miriam had done, so many years before, beside the Red Sea.

DAVID AND JONATHAN

I have told you that David, after killing the giant Goliath, was taken to King Saul. Now Saul had with him his son, who was called Jonathan. Jonathan was himself a brave soldier, and he admired David so much for his great deed that they at once became the best of friends.

"Jonathan loved David as his own soul." Jonathan took off his princely robe and gave it to David. He also gave him his sword, girdle and bow. This was the greatest honor one man could show to another. He did this so that every one should know how much he loved David.

Now Saul would not allow David to go home to his father's house. Wherever Saul went, there also was David. Saul placed him in command of the soldiers, and everywhere David was victorious.

It is said that when the king was worried or angry, the beautiful strains from David's harp at once soothed and quieted him.

The longer David was with the king, the stronger grew the love between David and Jonathan. When David became well known and beloved by all Israel, Saul grew jealous. Saul told Jonathan that he meant to kill David. Jonathan, because of his love for David,

DAVID AND JONATHAN

told him what his father wished to do. "Go, David," said he, "and hide thyself. I will go and talk to the king, my father." Then Jonathan spoke to Saul about the goodness of David. He reminded him of how he had killed Goliath, and had done so much for the people. Saul listened to these words, and said: "David shall not be slain." Then Jonathan brought David to Saul, and he lived with them as before.

Thus Jonathan, by saving the life of David, showed how great was his love for him. They loved each other so much that even now, when people speak of the great love that any two friends have for each other, they compare it with the love of David and Jonathan.

CPSIA information can be obtained at www.ICGtesting.com
Printed in the USA
BVOW071336171111
276302BV00001B/44/P